THE SECRETS OF ONLINE SUCCESS
MASTERING THE ART OF ONLINE ENTREPRENEURSHIP

2

Contents

3

Overview:

Businesses In the vast digital landscape of the 21st century, the allure of entrepreneurship beckons, and the path of online businesses serves as an enticing entryway for individuals who are looking for creative fulfillment in addition to financial independence. The omnipresence of the web has democratized admittance to business sectors, offering exceptional open doors for people to cut their specialties and assemble productive undertakings from the solace of their homes. Notwithstanding, leaving on this excursion requires cautious route through the horde of conceivable outcomes and difficulties that characterize the internet based business domain.

This extensive aide is planned as a guide, a signal enlightening the means toward finding a productive internet based business. Whether you are a carefully prepared business person hoping to progress into the web-based space or a rookie anxious to investigate the computerized wilderness, this guide will walk you through the mind boggling course of thought age, market examination, key preparation, and execution, all pointed toward transforming your yearnings into a flourishing internet based adventure.

Part 1: Self-Reflection: How Your Company Got Its Start Introspection is the first step on the journey. Prior to diving into the tremendous span of online business prospects, understanding oneself is significant.

What are your obsessions, interests, and abilities? Identifying these components not only ensures a long-lasting and fulfilling entrepreneurial experience but also forms the foundation of your venture. This section guides you through the course of self-revelation, empowering you to pinpoint what genuinely propels and drives you.

2nd Chapter: Statistical surveying - Exploring the Computerized Scene

In the unique universe of online business, keeping up to date with patterns and it is fundamental to distinguish worthwhile specialties. Part 2 dives into the complexities of statistical surveying, directing you on the most proficient method to examine contenders, recognize arising patterns, and approve the interest for your imminent business thought. Equipped with this information, you can pursue informed choices and position your endeavor decisively in the advanced commercial center.

Part 3: Crowd Recognizable proof - Associating with Your Clan

Understanding your ideal interest group is the foundation of an effective internet based business. This part accentuates the significance of characterizing your crowd, investigating their requirements, and distinguishing problem areas. By personally understanding your listeners' perspective, you can fit your items or administrations to address explicit difficulties, cultivating areas of strength for a reliable client base.

Section 4: Adaptation Systems - Clearing the Way to Income

Productivity is the soul of any business, and online endeavors are no exemption. Part 4 investigates different adaptation systems, from customary strategies like offering items or administrations to present day approaches like membership models and associate advertising. This part gives bits of knowledge into picking the right income model that lines up with your business objectives and client assumptions.

5th Chapter: Assess Assets - Setting the Foundation for Progress

No business can flourish without sufficient assets. Assessing your commitment to time, finances, and technical needs is made easier in Chapter 5. Understanding these elements is urgent for settling on informed conclusions about the possibility and maintainability of your internet based business. It guarantees that you are well-prepared for the upcoming journey.

Section 6: Building for the Future: Scalability and Sustainability A long-term online business is one that can grow and adapt to changing market dynamics. Part 6 spotlights on evaluating the adaptability of your plan of action and recognizing maintainability factors. It enables you to construct a venture that can withstand the test of time and encourages forward thinking.

7th Chapter: Lawful and Administrative Contemplations - Exploring the Legitimate Scene

In the computerized domain, lawful and administrative contemplations are frequently neglected however are basic for a business' life span. Part 7 gives direction on investigating lawful necessities, figuring out industry guidelines, and the significance of enrolling your business. By navigating the legal landscape, you can operate within the law, reduce risks, and build a trusted brand.

Section 8: Construct an Exceptional Offer - Catching everyone's eye

In a soaked web-based commercial center, separation is vital. Part 8 digs into making an interesting incentive that separates your business from rivals. This includes characterizing your image personality, making convincing informing, and building a brand that resounds with your ideal interest group.

Section 9: Make a Strategy - Graphing Your Course

A very much created strategy is the outline for progress. Section 9 diagrams the fundamental parts of a strategy, from characterizing objectives and goals to fostering a thorough showcasing procedure and monetary projections. A well-written business plan not only directs your actions but also helps you get investors or partners.

10th Chapter: Test Your Thought - From Idea to The real world

The change from ideation to execution includes testing your idea in reality. Part 10 investigates the idea of making a Base Practical Item (MVP), gathering input through beta testing, and emphasizing in light of client reactions. This iterative methodology guarantees your business develops to meet the advancing requirements of your main interest group.

Part 11: Construct Your Web-based Presence - Making a Computerized Personality

In the advanced time, your web-based presence is your customer facing facade. Section 11 gives experiences into fostering an expert site, utilizing online entertainment, and putting resources into Website streamlining (Web optimization). A hearty web-based presence is fundamental for drawing in and holding clients in the cutthroat web-based scene.

12th Chapter: Cultivating Relationships for Customer Acquisition and Retention Getting customers is just the beginning; holding them is the way to maintainable development. Section 12 investigates client procurement systems, from compelling promoting plans to methods for holding a devoted client base. Building solid associations with clients cultivates brand reliability and guarantees proceeded with progress.

Part 13: Investigation and Cycle - Information Driven Direction

In the computerized age, information is a strong resource. Part 13 accentuates the significance of executing examination devices, breaking down client conduct, and utilizing information driven bits of knowledge to emphasize and work on your business. Adjusting to changing patterns and client inclinations is fundamental for remaining serious.

Section 14: Adjust to Changes - Embracing Dynamism

The main consistent in the web-based business world is change. Part 14 urges you to remain informed about industry patterns, mechanical headways, and adjust to developing economic situations. Embracing change positions your business as a powerful player in the steadily moving computerized scene.

Section 15: Scale Your Business - Investigating Learning experiences

When your business has laid out its traction, the subsequent stage is scaling. Section 15 investigates development valuable open doors, including investigating new business sectors, taking into account organizations, and joint efforts. Scaling your business decisively guarantees supported development and long haul achievement.

Part 16: Monetary Administration - Exploring Financial Waters

Successful monetary administration is the foundation of a flourishing business. Part 16 aides you through observing income, overseeing costs, and making arrangements for development. Understanding the monetary parts of your business guarantees monetary security and strength.

17th Chapter: Ceaseless Learning - Developing with the Business

The internet based business scene is consistently advancing. Section 17 burdens the significance of nonstop getting the hang of, remaining refreshed on industry patterns, and putting resources into your abilities and information. You can position yourself as an entrepreneur who is well-informed and adaptable if you continue to learn.

18th Chapter: Networking and Developing Relationships: The Power of Connections In this digitally interconnected world, developing relationships is of the utmost importance. Section 18 investigates the advantages of going to industry occasions, meetings, and interfacing with tutors and friends. Organizing opens ways to joint effort, learning, and development.

All in all, this guide is your friend in the elating excursion of finding and building a beneficial web-based business. Every section is a venturing stone, giving bits of knowledge, instruments, and methodologies to explore the complex yet compensating scene of online business. By joining self-reflection, market experiences.

Part 1: Self-Reflection - The Beginning of Your Business

Leaving on the excursion of sending off a productive web-based business requires a profound plunge into self-reflection. This underlying part fills in as the foundation of your enterprising undertaking, directing you to uncover the foundations of your enthusiasm, abilities, and goals.

Grasping Your Interests:

The core of a fruitful web-based business frequently lies in adjusting your dare to your real advantages. Pause for a minute to introspect and recognize the exercises that light your excitement. Whether it's a side interest, a reason, or an industry you've forever been attracted to, recognizing your interests makes way for a business that feels less like work and more like a satisfying pursuit.

Evaluating Your Abilities and Skill:

A basic part of self-reflection includes a legit assessment of your abilities and skill. What are you incredibly great at? What remarkable abilities could you at any point use to make esteem? Perceiving your assets establishes the groundwork for a business where you can exhibit your capability and hang out in the packed web-based scene.

Distinguishing Issues You Need to Settle:

Business frequently flourishes with tackling issues. What difficulties or issues impact you? Distinguishing issues you are really roused to settle adjusts your business to a reason as well as positions you as an answer supplier according to your main interest group. Whether it's improving on a cycle, upgrading a help, or tending to a cultural need, these recognized issues can be the impetus for an effective web-based adventure.

Toward the finish of this part, you'll have a more clear comprehension of yourself, your interests, abilities, and the issues you are headed to settle. This mindfulness frames the bedrock whereupon your productive internet based business will be constructed, guaranteeing an endeavor that isn't just monetarily fulfilling yet in addition expressly satisfying.

Part 2: Market Research:

Navigating the Dynamic Terrain After laying the groundwork for a profitable online business through self-reflection, the next essential step is to navigate the dynamic terrain of market research. This part is intended to be your compass, directing you through the intricacies of understanding business sector patterns, dissecting contenders, and approving the interest for your planned business thought.

Distinguishing Patterns and Specialties:

Trends and emerging niches shape the ever-evolving online marketplace. In this part, you'll figure out how to recognize these patterns and specialties that current open doors for development and development. Whether it's gaining by arising advances, tending to moving purchaser inclinations, or taking advantage of underserved markets, perceiving patterns positions your business on the forefront.

Dissecting Contenders:

No endeavor exists in seclusion, and it is foremost to grasp your opposition. This piece of the part outfits you with systems to investigate contenders - from laid out players to arising new businesses. By evaluating their assets, shortcomings, and market situating, you can recognize holes, gain from their triumphs and disappointments, and cut out a particular space for your business.

Approving Interest for Your Thought:

Success is not dependent on a brilliant idea alone; it should satisfy a veritable need. You will be guided through validating the demand for your potential business in this section. Methods like overviews, interviews, and online apparatuses will be investigated, permitting you to measure crowd revenue and guarantee that your business thought reverberates with expected clients.

Toward the finish of this section, you'll have an extensive comprehension of the computerized scene pertinent to your business. Outfitted with bits of knowledge into market patterns, contender elements, and approved request, you'll be more ready to explore the intricacies of the internet based commercial center and position your endeavor for progress.

Part 3: understanding of your own motivations

With a clear understanding of your own motivations and a grasp of the market landscape, the focus now shifts to one of the most important factors in the success of your online business: Audience Identification -

Connecting with Your Tribe your crowd. This section dives into the craft of distinguishing your interest group, figuring out their necessities, and making an association that goes past conditional connections.

Identify Who You Want to Reach:

One-size-fits-everything is a misnomer in the web-based business world. This part directs you through the most common way of characterizing your main interest group with accuracy. Who are the people probably going to profit from your item or administration? What are your ideal customers' demographics, interests, and actions? By fostering a point by point persona, you can tailor your contributions to provide food explicitly to the requirements of your crowd.

Comprehend Client Needs and Problem areas:

Progress in the web-based domain frequently relies on how well you comprehend and address the requirements and trouble spots of your clients. This piece of the section investigates compelling procedures for social event bits of knowledge into client inclinations, difficulties, and wants. By distinguishing the trouble spots your crowd faces, you can tailor your business to give arrangements that really resound.

Construct a Relationship-Driven Approach:

Past simple exchanges, fabricating an enduring association with your crowd is fundamental. This part underscores the significance of developing a relationship-driven way to deal with business. Fostering a sense of community and loyalty enhances the overall value proposition of your online venture, whether through personalized communication, engaging content, or policies that focus on the customer.

Section 4: Adaptation Methodologies - Clearing the Way to Income

Having laid out a strong groundwork by grasping yourself, the market, and your crowd, the following pivotal stage in your excursion to a beneficial web-based business includes creating successful adaptation systems. In this section, we'll investigate different income models, from conventional ways to deal with creative strategies, to assist you with clearing the way to reasonable pay.

Investigate a variety of revenue models:

There is no universal strategy for monetization. This part digs into different income models, for example, item deals, administration expenses, and permitting. Understanding the complexities of each model engages you to pick the one that lines up with your business objectives and resounds with your main interest group. Whether you choose a one-time buy, a membership model, or a freemium procedure, choosing the right income model is a vital choice.

Consider Membership Administrations:

The membership model has acquired noticeable quality in the computerized time, giving a constant flow of income. This piece of the section investigates the subtleties of membership administrations, from estimating procedures to conveying reliable worth that keeps endorsers locked in. Whether you're offering select substance, programming, or an arranged encounter, a top notch membership model can make a steady revenue stream for your web-based business.

Assess Promoting and Member Showcasing:

Past direct deals, promoting and offshoot showcasing present worthwhile roads for adaptation. This segment guides you through the complexities of consolidating promotions on your foundation and collaborating with partners. Understanding how to figure out some kind of harmony between client experience and adaptation is fundamental, guaranteeing that your crowd stays connected with while producing income through essential associations and publicizing.

Toward the finish of this part, you'll have a far reaching comprehension of different adaptation systems and the capacity to pick the methodology that lines up with your plan of action. Compelling adaptation fills your endeavor's development as well as upgrades its manageability in the serious web-based scene.

Section 5: It's time to focus on the practical aspects of building and maintaining your online venture
Now that you have a clear vision of how your business will generate revenue. Evaluate Resources - Setting the Stage for Success Part 5 digs into the basic course of assessing the assets available to you, including time responsibility, spending plan contemplations, and the specialized prerequisites

expected to set the preparation for an effective web-based business.

Evaluate Your Time Responsibility:

Sending off and dealing with a web-based business requests a critical speculation of time. This segment prompts you to reasonably survey your accessibility. Is it true or not that you are seeking after this adventure full-time or as a side undertaking? Understanding your time responsibility helps in putting forth reasonable objectives, overseeing assumptions, and guaranteeing that you can devote the fundamental hours to cultivate your business' development.

Decide Spending plan and Speculation:

Monetary contemplations assume an essential part in any undertaking. This piece of the part directs you through deciding your financial plan and likely speculation. From beginning startup expenses for continuous costs, having an unmistakable monetary arrangement guarantees that you can support and scale your business without experiencing unanticipated difficulties. It covers angles like site improvement, showcasing, instruments, and other functional expenses.

Think about Specialized Prerequisites:

The web-based domain frequently requires a specific degree of specialized capability. The technical requirements that are necessary for the success of your online business are discussed in this section. Whether you really want a vigorous web based business stage, a substance the board framework, or explicit programming devices, understanding these necessities permits you to settle on informed choices and guarantee a consistent internet based presence.

Toward the finish of this section, you'll have a thorough outline of the assets expected to push your internet based adventure forward. Whether now is the right time, spending plan, or specialized expertise, this assessment stage establishes the groundwork for a sensible and feasible methodology, guaranteeing that you distribute assets really to accomplish your business targets.

Part 6: Versatility and Manageability - Working for What's to come

As you progress in your excursion to a productive web-based business, moving your concentration towards versatility and sustainability is basic. Part 6 is devoted to grasping the drawn out suitability of your endeavor, investigating methodologies for development, and guaranteeing your business is worked to endure the everyday hardships.

Assess Long haul Practicality:

Life span in the web-based business scene requires a sharp evaluation of your plan of action's suitability. This segment prompts you to consider factors, for example, changing business sector patterns, innovative progressions, and advancing client inclinations. By assessing the drawn out reasonability of your endeavor, you can proactively adjust to industry moves and position your business for supported achievement.

Consider Future Market Patterns:

Expecting future market patterns is a vital part of versatility. This piece of the part investigates strategies for remaining informed about industry changes, arising advances, and developing purchaser ways of behaving. By keeping a finger on the beat of market patterns, you can situate your business as a trailblazer, prepared to profit by new open doors and explore difficulties.

Survey Versatility of the Plan of action:

Adaptability is the capacity of your business to develop effectively without undermining its center capabilities. This segment guides you through surveying the adaptability of your plan of action. It doesn't matter if you want to diversify your revenue streams, enter new markets, or expand your product line; knowing how to scale your business will allow you to adapt to increased demand and take advantage of growth opportunities.

Toward the finish of this section, you'll have a key guide for building a business that isn't simply versatile to change yet additionally situated for supported development. The accentuation on long haul practicality, expectation of market patterns, and versatility guarantees that your web-based adventure is strong, flourishing, and prepared to embrace the valuable open doors that what's in store holds.

Part 7: Authentic and Regulatory Considerations - Investigating the Legal Scene

In the novel universe of online business, accomplishment depends on your thing or organization as well as on your ability to investigate the legitimate and authoritative scene. Section 7 is given to guiding you through the intricacies of genuine examinations, ensuring that your web based experience works inside the restrictions of the law and builds a foundation of trust and legitimacy.

Requirements for Research from the Law:

The real scene for online associations can vary basically dependent upon your region and the possibility of your undertaking. This part prompts you to examine and fathom the legal necessities pertinent to your business. Consistency with local regulations and guidelines is essential for a consistent and legal activity, from business enrollment to burden commitments.

Handle Industry Rules:

Certain organizations are reliant upon express rules and consistence standards. This piece of the segment examines the meaning of understanding industry-unequivocal rules that could apply to your web based business. Keeping up with these guidelines ensures that your business stays on favorable terms, whether they are information assurance regulations, permitting requirements, or industry-specific principles.

Register Your Association:

Formalizing your business through selection is a fundamental stage. This section provides insight into the process of incorporating your online business, whether as a sole proprietorship, LLC, or company. Enrolling your business updates its validness as well as gives explicit authentic protections and benefits.

You will have a thorough comprehension of the lawful and administrative contemplations that are crucial for the progress of your web-based business when this section is done. As well as safeguarding your organization, exploring the lawful scene with constancy and honesty fabricates trust among your accomplices and clients.

Section 8: Create a Unique Value Proposition

(UVP) to Stand Out from the Competition In today's crowded and competitive online environment, a UVP is what sets your company apart from the competition. Part 8 is committed to the specialty of making a convincing UVP that not just catches the consideration of your interest group yet additionally frames the bedrock of your image personality.

Separate Your Business from Rivals:

Understanding your rivals is critical, and this part directs you through the course of separation. What separates your business? Whether it's a special component, uncommon client care, or an unmistakable brand character, recognizing and featuring these differentiator's shapes the establishment for a solid UVP.

Define Your Identity as a Brand:

Your image character is something other than a logo; it's the pith of your business. This piece of the section investigates the components that add to a vigorous brand personality, including your image values, mission, and visual components. A durable brand character supports your UVP as well as encourages an association with your crowd.

Effectively Communicate Your Value Proposition:

It isn't sufficient to Art an UVP; Communication is essential. This part digs into methodologies for articulating your incentive across different touch points, from your site and promoting materials to online entertainment. Your audience will be aware of your business's unique value if you communicate clearly and consistently.

Toward the finish of this section, you'll have leveled up the ability of building an UVP that resounds with your interest group and separates your business in the serious web-based field. A convincing UVP draws in clients as well as structures the foundation of a brand that goes the distance.

9th Chapter: Make a Field-tested strategy - Graphing Your Course

A very much created field-tested strategy is the guide that directs your internet based adventure from origination to progress. Part 9 digs into the fundamental parts of an exhaustive strategy, assisting you with characterizing your objectives, foster a promoting system, and make monetary projections.

Outline Your Company's Objectives:

Putting forth clear and quantifiable objectives is the most important phase in making a marketable strategy. This part directs you through the most common way of framing your present moment and long haul goals. Whether it's accomplishing a specific degree of income, extending your client base, or sending off new items/administrations, obviously characterized objectives give guidance and inspiration for your business.

Foster a Showcasing Procedure:

A powerful showcasing procedure is essential for arriving at your interest group and laying out your image. This piece of the part investigates the vital components of a showcasing plan, including market situating, main interest group division, and special techniques. Making a promoting technique guarantees that your business is noticeable and reverberates with your target group.

Make budgetary projections:

Monetary projections are the foundation of your strategy, giving a guide to monetary achievement. This segment guides you through making sensible and information driven monetary projections, including income gauges, cost financial plans, and income explanations. Precise monetary projections assist with getting subsidizing as well as act as a device for observing and guiding your business' monetary wellbeing.

Toward the finish of this part, you'll have a far reaching field-tested strategy that fills in as an essential aide for your web-based adventure. Whether you're looking for venture, associations, or just a guide for your own direction, a very much created strategy is an important device in controlling your business towards progress.

Section 10: Test Your Thought - From Idea to The real world

With a distinct strategy close by, the following significant step is to progress from ideation to execution. Part 10 spotlights on testing your business thought in reality, gathering criticism, and repeating in light of client reactions.

Make a Base Suitable Item (MVP):

Before completely sending off your item or administration, foster a Base Reasonable Item (MVP). This segment guides you through the method involved with making a downsized form of your contribution that tends to the center necessities of your interest group. Sending off a MVP permits you to test the market with insignificant assets, assemble early criticism, and pursue informed choices for the full-scale send off.

Collect Information from Beta Testing:

Beta testing is a urgent stage in refining your contribution in light of genuine client encounters. The methods for selecting beta testers, collecting feedback, and analyzing results are examined in this section of the chapter. The experiences acquired during this stage assist with distinguishing regions for development and guarantee that your end result/administration lives up to the assumptions of your crowd.

Emphasize In view of Client Reactions:

The iterative cycle is vital to refining your business thought. This segment underscores the significance of effectively paying attention to client reactions, whether through overviews, client interviews, or examination. Emphasizing in view of this criticism permits you to make essential changes, upgrade client experience, and guarantee that your contribution adjusts intimately with client needs.

Toward the finish of this section, you'll have changed your business thought from idea to the real world, tried its suitability on the lookout, and iterated in light of significant client criticism. This active methodology guarantees that your eventual outcome or administration isn't just generally welcomed yet additionally situated for progress in the serious web-based scene.

Segment 11: Create Your Web based Presence - Making a Mechanized Person

In the mechanized period, a strong online presence is key to the result of any business. Segment 11 helpers you through the most well-known approach to spreading out and supporting your electronic character, wrapping the improvement of a specialist webpage, using on the web amusement, and placing assets into Site smoothing out (Website streamlining).

Establish a Expert Website:

Your site is by and large the foremost affiliation potential clients have with your business. This part explores the fundamental parts of building a specialist and simple to utilize site. From normal course and persuading substance to responsive arrangement, your site is a modernized client confronting exterior that reflects the pith of your picture.

Impact Virtual Diversion:

Online diversion stages offer astonishing resources for attracting with your group and broadening your reach. This piece of the part plunges into procedures for using electronic diversion effectively. From picking the right stages for your vested party to making attracting blissful and developing neighborhood, strong virtual diversion presence redesigns brand detectable quality and client cooperation.

Make a bet on Web optimization:

Webpage plan improvement (Web streamlining) is urgent for ensuring that your business is discoverable on the web. This section explains how to optimize your website for search engines, select relevant catchphrases, and use both on-page and off-page Web optimization techniques. A strong Website improvement foundation deals with your webpage's detectable quality as well as attracts regular busy time gridlock.

Close to the completion of this part, you'll have spread out a persuading web based presence that displays your business to the mechanized world. Whether through a specialist website, dynamic virtual diversion responsibility, or smoothed out Web composition upgrade practices, your mechanized character transforms into major areas of strength for an in attracting and holding clients in the serious electronic scene.

Area 12: Client Getting and Support - Creating Associations

With your web based presence spread out, the middle developments to acquiring and holding clients. From the production of an extensive showcasing system to the execution of strategies for client maintenance, successful techniques for gaining clients are analyzed in Section 12.

Cultivate a Displaying Plan:

A thoroughly examined promoting methodology is fundamental for getting new clients to your business. In this section, you'll learn how to put together a comprehensive marketing strategy. From perceiving your ideal vested party to picking the right advancing channels, a convincing plan ensures that your message contacts the ideal people and makes interest in your things or organizations.

Do Client Getting Systems:

Client obtainment is the most well-known approach to changing over logical clients into paying clients. The advanced marketing, content marketing, and force to be reckoned with joint efforts are just a few of the client procurement strategies examined in this section. You can fit your technique to the inclinations and activities of your interest group by being familiar with the different channels and methodologies.

Base on Client Support:

While getting new clients is crucial, holding existing clients is likewise critical for upheld business accomplishment. This section plunges into methods for client upkeep, for instance, devotion programs, altered correspondence, and amazing client care. Building strong relationship with your ongoing client base develops brand faithfulness and supports go over business.

Close to the completion of this part, you'll have a decent method for managing client obtainment and support. Whether through assigned displaying tries or tweaked upkeep systems, creating strong relationship with your clients drives starting arrangements as well as spreads out a foundation for long stretch advancement in the electronic business scene.

Part 13: Assessment and Accentuation - Data Driven Route

In the data driven universe of online business, using assessment and accentuation is critical for relentless improvement. Section 13 plunges into the meaning of data driven autonomous course, researching how assessment devices can be used to analyze client lead and guide the iterative cycle.

Use apparatuses for investigation:

Understanding client direct and responsibility is fundamental to refining your web based business. This section looks into how examination tools like Google Examination are used to gather important data. Following estimations like site traffic, client economics, and change rates gives pieces of information that enlighten key decisions and progressions.

Examine Customer Behavior:

One of the main parts of further developing your web-based presence is deciphering client conduct. You will figure out how to examine client cooperation's, for example, online visits, navigate rates, and client venture examination, in this segment of the part. By understanding how clients attract with your establishment, you can perceive areas for advancement and creator your commitments to meet their tendencies.

Underline and Move along:

The iterative cooperation is the heartbeat of a powerful electronic business. This portion underlines the meaning of using examination pieces of information to rehash and work on your things, organizations, and overall client experience. Whether it's refining web structure, changing exhibiting systems, or overhauling thing incorporates, reliable cycle ensures that your business stays material and responsive to changing business area components.

Around the completion of this part, you'll be capable at using examination to enlighten your dynamic communication and drive relentless improvement. The marriage of data driven encounters with the iterative mindset ensures that your electronic business stays agile, flexible, and arranged for upheld improvement in the reliably progressing mechanized scene.

Part 14: Embracing dynamism and versatility

Are crucial for long haul progress in the unique web-based business climate. Segment 14 bright lights on the meaning of embracing change, staying informed about industry designs, and proactively changing your approaches to meet progressing monetary circumstances.

Stay Informed About Industry Examples:

This section examines methods for staying informed, such as industry announcements, planning events, and online gatherings. You position your company to anticipate and adapt to changes by staying up to date on upcoming developments, shifts in customer behavior, and significant occurrences.

Make the Change to Mechanical Headways:

Development is a primary force in the improvement of online associations. This piece of the part focuses on the need to conform to imaginative movements. Whether it's incorporating new instruments, embracing innovative stages, or using the latest programming, a very much educated approach ensures that your business stays powerful, relentless, and at the extreme front line of industry designs.

Turn and Emphasize:

A portion of the time, variety requires more than slow changes - it requires key turns. This segment digs into the possibility of cycle and key turning, taking a gander at situations in which a central change in the contributions or plan of action may be required. Being accessible to accentuation and turn ensures that your business can make the most of new possibilities and investigate troubles effectively.

Close to the completion of this segment, you'll have encouraged a viewpoint of adaptability, understanding that change isn't a risk yet an opportunity for improvement. Embracing dynamism positions your electronic business to prosper in a persistently creating environment, ensuring that you stay solid and responsive to the consistently changing solicitations of the market.

72

Part 15: Scale Your Business - Researching Important growth opportunities

Having spread out areas of strength for an and investigated the complexities of the web based business scene, the open door has shown up to explore streets for scaling your undertaking. Segment 15 is dedicated to getting a handle on growth opportunities, expanding your degree, and conclusively raising your business higher than at any other time.

Research New Business areas:

One of the essential frameworks for scaling your business is to explore new business areas. This section guides you through the course of market expansion, whether it incorporates reaching an overall group, zeroing in on specialty exhibits, or improving your thing or organization commitments. Examining new business areas opens up streets for extended pay and business advancement.

Ponder Affiliations and Composed endeavors:

Facilitated endeavors and affiliations can areas of strength for be for improvement. The benefits of forming key alliances with various organizations, powerhouses, or associations are examined in this section. By using reciprocal characteristics and shared swarms, affiliations can heighten your reach, update legitimacy, and open new opportunities for growth.

Evaluate Expanding or Approving:

For explicit game plans, differentiating or allowing can be a plausible way corresponding. The elements to consider while permitting your labor and products to other people or diversifying your business are talked about in this part. You can recreate your fruitful model and grow your image's presence utilizing these techniques without bearing the full expense of development.

At the end of this section, you will have learned how to scale your business in a key and practical way. Whether through market expansion, facilitated endeavors, or creative game plans, examining growth opportunities ensures that your web based experience forms into a generous and prospering endeavor.

Part 16: Exploring Financial Waters:

Monetary Administration Powerful financial management is the foundation of a successful business. Segment 16 provides guidance on noticing pay, regulating expenses, and making game plans for advancement, ensuring that your web based business remains areas of strength for financially.

Screen Play:

Your organization's income is its backbone, so watching out for it is fundamental. Making income declarations, improving invoicing procedures, and implementing installment terms that achieve some kind of balance between costs and income are all topics covered in this section. Your organization will actually want to meet its monetary commitments and make the most of learning experiences assuming its income is sound.

Carefully Monitor Costs:

Keeping up with benefit requires reasonable cost administration. This piece of the segment jumps into methodology for controlling costs, organizing great terms with suppliers, and perceiving areas where practical efficiency can be gotten to a higher level. Key expense organization ensures that your business works successfully and supports efficiency.

Development Plan:

As your business scales, essential financial organizing ends up being dynamically critical. This portion guides you through the technique associated with making money related projections, anticipating advancement, and getting funding if vital. A well-organized financial plan gives investors, partners, and stakeholders confidence and supports your growth initiatives.

Close to the completion of this segment, you'll have a careful perception of money related organization guidelines custom fitted to the unique challenges of a web based business. Convincing financial management is an essential component of creating a cost-effective and efficient online experience, whether you're looking for speculation, planning for expansion, or everyday finances.

Part 17: Interminable Learning - The Way to Strength

In the consistently propelling scene of online business, the outing doesn't end; it changes into a steady example of learning and change. Section 17 is dedicated to the tenet of persistent learning, examining how staying informed, acquiring new skills, and adopting a development mindset are essential for long-term success.

Stay Informed About Industry Changes:

Staying instructed is the foundation in regards to unending learning. This part explores systems for staying up with the latest with industry changes, emerging advances, and moving purchaser approaches to acting. Whether through industry dispersions, online social events, or frameworks organization events, persistent care positions you to change proactively to changes in the business environment.

Acquire New Skills and Knowledge:

The electronic scene is dynamic, requiring a promise to acquiring new capacities. This piece of the part jumps into the meaning of capacity improvement and reliable tutoring. Whether it's ruling new developments, learning about emerging examples, or working on drive capacities, a guarantee to getting new data ensures that you stay a skilled and flexible business pioneer.

Embrace an Improvement Mindset:

An improvement viewpoint is the underpinning of predictable learning. The possibility of a development outlook is the focal point of this segment, which underscores the conviction that knowledge and capacities can be created through difficult work and commitment. A development mindset fosters strength, adaptability, and a willingness to tackle new challenges—important perspectives for exploring the unique world of online business.

Around the completion of this part, you'll have embraced the perspective of relentless progressing as a fundamental piece of your imaginative outing. The commitment to staying informed, acquiring new capacities, and fostering an improvement mindset ensures that you make due as well as prosper in the reliably changing scene of online business.

Part 18: Association and Collect Associations - The Power of Affiliations

In the interconnected universe of online business, frameworks organization and relationship-building are significant contraptions for advancement and accomplishment. Section 18 dives into the art of building critical affiliations, whether with individual business visionaries, industry trained professionals, or anticipated clients.

Participate in Electronic Organizations:

Participating in web-based networks relevant to your industry is an effective strategy for interacting with like-minded individuals. This section researches the upsides of partaking in conversations, virtual amusement get-togethers, and other electronic organizations. You not just form an organization of strong associations and grow your insight by sharing bits of knowledge, getting clarification on some things, and partaking in conversations.

Attend both in-person and online events:

Both in-person and online events provide opportunities to coordinate with experts, anticipated partners, and clients. This piece of the part researches strategies for going to online courses, social occasions, and meetups. Whether on the web or detached, events give a phase to spreading out affiliations, sharing your dominance, and empowering associations that can incite joint endeavors and business important entryways.

Foster Relationship with Forces to be reckoned with:

Powerhouses in your industry can expect a pressing part in expanding your reach. This section guides you through the most widely recognized approach to recognizing and creating relationship with forces to be reckoned with. Whether through joint endeavors, affiliations, or shared content, building relationship with forces to be reckoned with can overhaul your picture detectable quality and legitimacy.

Close to the completion of this segment, you'll have a device compartment for fruitful frameworks organization and relationship-working in the electronic space. Whether you're taking part in online organizations, going to events, or collaborating with forces to be reckoned with, building critical affiliations is a fundamental asset that drives your web based business forward.

www.ingramcontent.com/pod-product-compliance
Lightning Source LLC
Chambersburg PA
CBHW050044260726
48658CB00005B/1762